LOST AND FOUND

BIBLE TRIVIA FOR THE SEARCHING SOUL

TAMELA HANCOCK MURRAY

BARBOUR BOOKS
An Imprint of Barbour Publishing, Inc.

LOST AND FOUND

© 2002 by Barbour Publishing, Inc.

ISBN 1-58660-498-8

All Scripture quotations, unless otherwise noted, are taken from the King James Version of the Bible.

Published by Barbour Books, an imprint of Barbour Publishing, Inc., P.O. Box 719, Uhrichsville, Ohio 44683, www.barbourbooks.com

 Member of the
Evangelical Christian
Publishers Association

Printed in the United States of America.
5 4 3 2

INTRODUCTION

Greetings! I am Saul of Tarsus, better known as the apostle Paul. As an unsaved person, I was one of the most spiritually lost men of the Bible. I was a learned Jewish man. My faith was such that I persecuted Christians. I had no idea I was really lost. I was wandering through a wasteland, the spiritual equivalent of the wilderness the Israelites journeyed through on their way to Canaan.

No one would have thought I would become a Christian, let alone preach the gospel to the Gentiles, take three missionary journeys, and even go to prison for my newfound faith. But then I met Jesus on the road to Damascus. He showed me the true path—that He is the only way to God the Father. *Jesus saith unto him, I am the way, the truth, and the life: no man cometh unto the Father, but by me* (John 14:6).

As you journey through this book, you will meet other people whose stories appear in the

Bible. Their lives were far from flawless. Many had to overcome great sin before they could find the narrow road. Others knew the Lord but wandered off the righteous path. Their stories show how they entered into fellowship with Him once more.

Perhaps you know someone who seems lost. Perhaps you aren't feeling as close to the Lord as you would like. If so, answering the questions in this book will give you hope. No matter how far off the course we ramble, we are never out of God's reach.

Scoring:

12-15 correct – You're on the right path!

8-11 correct – You're heading in the right
    direction.

4-7 correct – You shouldn't have taken that
    left turn. Refer to your guidebook, the
    Bible, to get back on course.

0-3 correct – Inexperienced travelers need not
    worry. The Lord has left us with His per-
    fect Guidebook. Read and study the pas-
    sages covered by the quiz and try again.
    Before you know it, you'll be an expert
    navigator!

NOTE: The answers for each section follow
    the final question of that section.

Quiz 1

Greetings! Good to see you here in Jerusalem. Although I was a Pharisee, a man of learning, I was lost spiritually. I thought I was serving God by hating Jesus Christ and His followers. But because of Christ's love for me, I found my way along the road to Damascus.

I am _____.

▶▶   1. When Paul was lost, he:

     a. persecuted Christians
     b. witnessed Jesus' crucifixion
     c. took three missionary journeys
     d. asked Timothy for a map to
     Damascus

▶▶   2. True or False: Paul is mentioned in John's gospel.

▶▶   3. Who gave Paul permission to bring Christians to Jerusalem for persecution?

▶▶   4. *And the Lord said, I am* _____ *whom thou persecutest: it is hard for thee to kick against the pricks.*

▶▶ 5. Acts 13:47 reads, *For so hath the Lord commanded us, saying, I have set thee to be a light of the Gentiles, that thou shouldest be for salvation unto the ends of the earth.* This is the same as a verse in the Book of:

    a. Genesis
    b. Deuteronomy
    c. Isaiah
    d. Jude

▶▶ 6. When Paul was brought up on unspecified charges by the Jews, to which king did he tell his life story?

▶▶ 7. Because of Paul's testimony, this king:

    a. grew angrier than ever
    b. vowed to kill the Jews who opposed Paul
    c. built a temple to the Lord
    d. almost became a Christian

▶▶ 8. Paul wrote to the Romans, *For I am not _____ of the gospel of Christ: for it is the power of God unto salvation to every one that believeth; to the Jew first, and also to the Greek.*

▶▶ 9. Paul wrote that he fed the Corinthians:

a. meat   c. bread
b. water   d. milk

▶▶ 10. How many letters did Paul write to the Corinthians?

▶▶ 11. Paul tells the Galatians that the just shall live by:

a. the law
b. their wits
c. faith
d. alms given to the church

▶ ▶ 12. Ephesians 4:26 cautions: *Be ye angry, and sin not: let not the sun go down upon your* _____.

▶ ▶ 13. Paul advised the Colossians to temper their speech with grace and season it with:

   a. fire   c. salt
   b. love   d. pepper

▶ ▶ 14. Paul called Timothy his:

   a. son in the faith
   b. brother in the faith
   c. fellow apostle
   d. yoke

▶ ▶ 15. True or False: Paul was in prison when he wrote to Philemon.

QUIZ 1 ANSWERS

I am Paul, or Saul of Tarsus.

1. a. persecuted Christians (Acts 9:1–2)
2. False
3. The high priest (Acts 9:1–2)
4. Jesus (Acts 9:5)
5. c. Isaiah 49:6: *And he said, It is a light thing that thou shouldest be my servant to raise up the tribes of Jacob, and to restore the preserved of Israel: I will also give thee for a light to the Gentiles, that thou mayest be my salvation unto the end of the earth.*
6. King Agrippa (Acts 26:1)
7. d. almost became a Christian (Acts 26:28)
8. Ashamed (Romans 1:16)
9. d. milk (1 Corinthians 3:2)
10. Two
11. c. faith (Galatians 3:11)
12. Wrath
13. c. salt (Colossians 4:6)
14. a. son in the faith (1 Timothy 1:2)
15. True (Philemon 1:1)

QUIZ 1 WRAP-UP

Congratulations are in order if you answered at least twelve questions correctly.

I must leave you now as I see another man of the Bible approaching. May God bless you as you continue on your journey.

**Therefore being justified by faith,
we have peace with God
through our Lord Jesus Christ.**
ROMANS 5:1

Quiz Two

God asked me to do something I didn't want to do. Instead of obeying, I ran away in hopes that I would become lost. Thankfully, He showed me the error of my ways. My heart was changed, and I was found again.

I am _____.

▶▶ 1. Jonah was asked to go to Nineveh by whom?

▶▶ 2. Jonah was instructed to tell the Ninevites that:

  a. they had found grace in the eyes of the Lord
  b. the Lord was against their wickedness
  c. they were to build an ark to prepare for an oncoming flood
  d. they were to build a temple in God's honor

▶▶ 3. Jonah boarded a ship to Tarshish because:

  a. Tarshish was on the way to Nineveh
  b. he had been told to take a priest from Tarshish with him
  c. he wanted to flee from the Lord
  d. he needed a catch of fish to take along as food

▶▶ 4. What happened to the sea after Jonah boarded the ship?

▶▶ 5. True or False: The Bible says that Jonah was swallowed by a whale.

▶▶ 6. *But I will sacrifice unto thee with the voice of thanksgiving; I will pay that that I have vowed.* _____ *is of* the LORD.

▶▶ 7. Jonah told the Ninevites that they had how many days left before God would destroy them?

▶▶   8. After the Ninevites heard the message
      from God delivered by Jonah, they:

      a. threw Jonah out of town
      b. stoned Jonah
      c. fasted and wore sackcloth
      d. proclaimed the Lord was greater than
         Baal

▶▶   9. True or False: The king of Nineveh
      resisted God's call to repentance.

▶▶   10. Nineveh's repentance angered Jonah
      because:

      a. Nineveh wasn't part of his own
         country
      b. his ex-wife lived in Nineveh
      c. success meant he would be required
         to join the priesthood
      d. the Ninevites didn't invite him to
         their revival service

▶▶ 11. True or False: Jonah asked God to take his life.

▶▶ 12. Why did Jonah remain near Nineveh?

▶▶ 13. The plant that shaded Jonah as he waited was a:

a. cactus   c. gourd
b. Venus fly trap d. cypress tree

▶▶ 14. The plant was destroyed by:

a. a bolt of lightning
b. a worm
c. a lack of flies to eat
d. harsh sunlight

▶▶ 15. God made and destroyed the plant to show Jonah what?

QUIZ 2 ANSWERS

I am Jonah.

1. The Lord (Jonah 1:1–2)
2. b. the Lord was against their wickedness (Jonah 1:2).
3. c. he wanted to flee from the Lord (Jonah 1:3).
4. A great wind caused the sea to rage (Jonah 1:4).
5. False. He was swallowed by a fish. (Jonah 1:17).
6. *Salvation* (Jonah 2:9)
7. Forty (Jonah 3:4)
8. c. fasted and wore sackcloth (Jonah 3:5)
9. False (Jonah 3:6). For his entire decree, see verses 6–9.
10. a. Nineveh wasn't part of his own country (Jonah 4:2).
11. True (Jonah 4:3)
12. He wanted to see what would happen to the city (Jonah 4:5).
13. c. gourd (Jonah 4:6)
14. b. a worm (Jonah 4:7)
15. *Then said the LORD, Thou hast had pity on the gourd, for the which thou hast not laboured, neither madest it grow; which came up in a night, and perished in a night: And should not I spare Nineveh, that great city, wherein are more than sixscore thousand persons that cannot discern between their right hand and their left hand; and also much cattle?* (Jonah 4:10–11)

QUIZ 2 WRAP-UP

I trust you didn't have to "fish" too hard to find answers to my questions! Farewell, my friend—I hope you've found our time together beneficial. Your next traveling companion awaits. He has much to teach you.

> But I will sacrifice unto thee
> with the voice of thanksgiving;
> I will pay that that I have vowed.
> Salvation is of the LORD.
> JONAH 2:9

Quiz 3

I appear in a well-known story of the New Testament. The account of my journey illustrates God's true love for those who are lost. As the Lord will accept the lost with loving arms when they repent, so my father accepted me once I returned home.

I am _____.

▶ ▶   1. True or False: The story of the prodigal son appears in two Gospels, Luke and Matthew.

▶ ▶   2. Who told this story?

▶ ▶   3. True or False: This story is based on the lives of Old Testament brothers, Jacob and Esau.

▶ ▶   4. How many sons did the father have?

▶ ▶   5. Is the story of the prodigal son the same story as the story of the two sons that appears in Matthew 21:28–32?

▶▶ 6. The younger son received his newfound
        wealth from:

        a. gambling
        b. taking his inheritance early
        c. marrying well
        d. hard work

▶▶ 7. After becoming wealthy, the younger
        son went to:

        a. Jerusalem
        b. a far country
        c. the nearest large city
        d. Nineveh

▶▶ 8. After the son ran out of money, the
        land where he lived experienced:

        a. plague   c. famine
        b. war   d. flood

▶▶ 9. *And he went and joined himself to a citizen of that country; and he sent him into his fields to feed* _____.

▶▶ 10. The son finally decided to repent as a result of his:

    a. loss of friends
    b. knowledge that his father would forgive him
    c. love for the virgin he left behind
    d. hunger

▶▶ 11. Did the son believe he could return home and take back his position as son?

▶▶ 12. True or False: As soon as the father saw the son returning, he ran to greet him.

▶▶ 13. The father gave the son:

a. a ring   c. shoes
b. a robe   d. all of the above

▶▶ 14. True or False: The older brother was
        upset that the father celebrated his
        younger brother's return by killing the
        fatted calf.

▶▶ 15. *It was meet that we should make merry,
        and be glad: for this thy brother was dead,
        and is alive again; and was _____,
        and is found.*

QUIZ 3 ANSWERS

I am the prodigal son.

1. False. It only appears in Luke.
2. The Lord Jesus Christ
3. False. Jesus does not tell us whether the story is based on real people.
4. Two (Luke 15:11)
5. No. Explore Matthew 21:28–32 for a lesson on believers and the Kingdom of God.
6. b. taking his inheritance early (Luke 15:12)
7. b. a far country (Luke 15:13)
8. c. famine (Luke 15:14)
9. Swine (Luke 15:15)
10. d. hunger (Luke 15:17–18)
11. No. He planned to ask if his father would accept him as a hired servant (Luke 15:19).
12. True (Luke 15:20)
13. d. all of the above (Luke 15:22)
14. True (Luke 15:28–30)
15. Lost (Luke 15:32)

QUIZ 3 WRAP-UP

So, were you able to answer at least twelve of my questions? I hope so, because my story should be a great encouragement to you: If you're lost, you, too, can be found! Now I hear footsteps approaching. Go and see who is coming to meet you.

**There is joy in the presence of
the angels of God over
one sinner that repenteth.**
LUKE 15:10

Quiz 4

I was a runaway slave who was spiritually lost, but the apostle Paul led me to Christ. In an epistle (that's a "letter" in your modern language), Paul asked my master to forgive me.

I am _____.

▶▶ 1. The passage about Onesimus is found in which epistle written by Paul?

▶▶ 2. True or False: Paul was in prison when he wrote this letter.

▶▶ 3. Why was Paul in trouble with the authorities at this time?

▶▶ 4. Paul was with:

   a. Timothy   c. Epaphras
   b. Philemon's brother   d. Felix

▶▶ 5. In the epistle, Paul calls the recipient a:

   a. church elder
   b. lady of the church
   c. dearly beloved and fellowlabourer
   d. son in Christ

▶▶ 6. When Paul describes Onesimus as his son *whom I have begotten in my bonds*, he means that Onesimus was:

a. the product of an unhappy marriage
b. the son of Paul's unsaved wife
c. a son Paul begot before he knew Christ
d. led by Paul to Christ while Paul was in prison

▶▶ 7. Onesimus was:

a. one of the seventy-two ordained by Jesus
b. a slave owned by Philemon
c. a young man who fell asleep as Paul preached
d. a Roman centurion

▶▶ 8. True or False: Paul was writing to say he was sending Onesimus back home.

▶▶ 9. How was Onesimus helping Paul?

▶▶ 10. *For perhaps he therefore departed for a season, that thou shouldest receive him for ever; Not now as a servant, but above a servant, a _____ beloved, specially to me, but how much more unto thee, both in the flesh, and in the Lord?*

▶▶ 11. If Onesimus owes Philemon money, Paul says the debt will be repaid by:

   a. Onesimus
   b. Paul
   c. Jesus
   d. Timothy

▶▶ 12. True or False: Paul had also brought Philemon to Christ.

▶▶ 13. True or False: Paul has confidence that Philemon will obey his instructions.

▶▶ 14. Paul asks Philemon to prepare him a:

      a. lodging
      b. fine meal
      c. key to unlock his chains
      d. donkey for his travels

▶▶ 15. Paul asked Philemon to prepare him this because:

      a. he expected to be released soon
      b. prison food was undesirable
      c. he planned his escape
      d. Philemon lived many miles away

QUIZ 4 ANSWERS

I am Onesimus.

1. Philemon
2. True (Philemon 1:9)
3. For his allegiance to Jesus Christ (Philemon 1:9)
4. c. Epaphras (Philemon 1:23)
5. c. dearly beloved and fellowlabourer (Philemon 1:1)
6. d. led by Paul to Christ while Paul was in prison (Philemon 1:10)
7. b. a slave owned by Philemon (Philemon 1:16)
8. True (Philemon 1:12)
9. He was ministering to Paul (Philemon 1:13).
10. Brother (Philemon 1:15–16)
11. b. Paul (Philemon 1:19)
12. True (Philemon 1:19)
13. True (Philemon 1:21)
14. a. lodging (Philemon 1:22)
15. a. he expected to be released soon (Philemon 1:22)

Quiz 4 Wrap-up

So how did you fare with my questions? If you answered at least twelve correctly, you are "free" to continue your journey. Hark! I see a shepherd and his flock approaching in the distance. I must go and leave you to his company.

The grace of our Lord Jesus Christ be with your spirit. Amen.
PHILEMON 1:25

Quiz 5

I am an animal caretaker of the Middle East, in Jesus' day. I am responsible for the life of every woolly creature in my care. If I lose one, I must explain this to my master. That's why I'm so happy when I find one that is lost.

Likewise, God is happy when a lost soul returns to Him!

I appear in the story of the lost

_____.

▶▶ 1. When Jesus was teaching, a group of
        Pharisees complained that his audience
        consisted of:

        a. the liberal elite
        b. the illiterate
        c. apostates
        d. sinners

▶▶ 2. Jesus answered them with stories called
        what?

▶▶ 3. True or False: The story of the Lost
        Sheep can be found in Matthew and
        Luke.

▶▶ 4. *What man of you, having an hundred
        sheep, if he lose one of them, doth not leave
        the ninety and nine in the wilderness, and
        go after that which is lost, until he
        _____ it?*

▶▶ 5. When the sheep is found, the shepherd rejoices and lays it:

    a. in the manger
    b. upon the hay
    c. by its mother
    d. on his shoulders

▶▶ 6. True or False: The shepherd goes even further by calling together friends and neighbors to celebrate.

▶▶ 7. Jesus said there is more joy in heaven over one sinner who repents than:

    a. the birth of a first son
    b. ninety-nine who need no repentance
    c. nine ladies dancing
    d. the dawn of one's wedding day

▶▶ 8. Jesus told another story of an object that was lost. What is it?

▶▶ 9. Soon after Jesus told stories about the lost, he shared a parable about the:

    a. wheat and the tares
    b. great supper
    c. unjust servant
    d. mustard seed

▶▶ 10. After the Pharisees heard the stories, they:

    a. derided Jesus
    b. asked Him to explain them
    c. saw some of their own repent
    d. plotted then and there to kill Him

▶▶ 11. They did this because they:

    a. coveted the possessions of others
    b. were embarrassed by their lack of understanding
    c. were moved by the Lord's wisdom
    d. hated His goodness

▶ ▶ 12. True or False: The illustrations of the lost sheep and the lost coin show how God seeks sinners.

▶ ▶ 13. What disciple later wrote that God "is not willing that any should perish"?

▶ ▶ 14. *And he said unto them, Ye are they which justify yourselves before men; but God knoweth your hearts: for that which is highly esteemed among men is _____ in the sight of God.*

▶ ▶ 15. Name the famous Psalm that says, *The LORD is my shepherd; I shall not want.*

QUIZ 5 ANSWERS

I appear in the story of the lost sheep.

1. d. sinners (Luke 15:1–2)
2. Parables
3. True (Matthew 18:12–14 and Luke 15:4–7)
4. Find (Luke 15:4)
5. d. on his shoulders (Luke 15:5)
6. True (Luke 15:6). Compare to the celebration in the parable of the prodigal son.
7. b. ninety-nine who need no repentance (Luke 15:7)
8. A coin (Luke 15:8)
9. c. unjust servant (Luke 16:1–13)
10. a. derided Jesus (Luke 16:14)
11. a. coveted the possessions of others (Luke 16:14)
12. True
13. Peter (2 Peter 3:9)
14. Abomination (Luke 16:15)
15. Psalm 23

QUIZ 5 WRAP-UP

Is it not a wonderful thing to be desired by God?
If you answered at least twelve questions correctly,
you may continue your journey. Look—another
follower of the one true God is waiting to test
your knowledge. I wish you well.

**For the Son of man is come to save
that which was lost.**
MATTHEW 18:11

Quiz 6

Shalom. I am one of a group of people whom God loves. I am grieved to admit that my people have not always been faithful to Jehovah God. The Bible shows that we were often impatient and willful, and that our faith floundered at the very times it needed to be strongest. Still, the Scriptures show that under good leadership, we often returned to the one true God.

I am an _____.

▶▶ 1. Immediately before the Israelites left their bondage in Egypt, the Lord established what remembrance that the Jewish people still observe?

▶▶ 2. True or False: Immediately after the exodus, the Israelites believed in God and in the leadership of His servant, Moses.

▶▶ 3. After the Lord brought His people out of Egypt, they immediately:

   a. celebrated Passover
   b. prayed
   c. built a temple
   d. sang and danced

▶▶ 4. When the people first questioned the leadership of Moses, they had been three days without:

     a. water   c. meat
     b. manna   d. shelter

▶▶ 5. *And when they came to Marah, they could not drink of the waters of Marah, for they were _____: therefore the name of it was called Marah.*

▶▶ 6. The Lord asked the Israelites for one thing. What was it?

▶▶ 7. True or False: The people complained about having no meat.

▶▶ 8. *And all the people answered together, and said, All that the _____ hath spoken we will do.*

▶▶ 9. True or False: The people promised to obey all of God's laws.

▶▶ 10. The people strayed when Moses:

    a. questioned whether or not the Lord is true

    b. was unable to make the waters at Marah sweet

    c. murdered an Egyptian and fled

    d. delayed his return from the mountaintop

▶▶ 11. When Aaron discovered the Israelites were building an idol, he:

    a. told them to stop

    b. said the Lord would surely punish them

    c. helped them build it

    d. suggested they build even more idols

▶▶ 12. True or False: After the Israelites built the idol, the Lord sent them a plague.

▶▶ 13. True or False: When the people repented, they donated their riches and talents to the Lord.

▶▶ 14. What did the people build to honor the Lord?

▶▶ 15. True or False: The project was not completed in Moses' lifetime.

QUIZ 6 ANSWERS

I am an Israelite.

1. Passover (Exodus 12:43)
2. True (Exodus 14:31)
3. d. sang and danced (Exodus 15:1–21)
4. a. water (Exodus 15:22, 24)
5. Bitter (Exodus 15:23)
6. Obedience. *And said, If thou wilt diligently hearken to the voice of the LORD thy God, and wilt do that which is right in his sight, and wilt give ear to his commandments, and keep all his statutes, I will put none of these diseases upon thee, which I have brought upon the Egyptians: for I am the LORD that healeth thee.* (Exodus 15:26)
7. True (Exodus 16:3)
8. LORD (Exodus 19:8)
9. True (Exodus 24:3)
10. d. delayed his return from the mountaintop (Exodus 32:1)
11. c. helped them build it (Exodus 32:3–5)
12. True (Exodus 32:35)
13. True (Exodus 35)
14. A tabernacle (Exodus 35:21)
15. False (Exodus 39:32)

QUIZ 6 WRAP-UP

My best advice for you is this: Don't follow our example. But if you do stray from the Lord's path, be confident that He will always welcome you back. Behold, a foreigner approaches. I bid you farewell.

**The children of Israel
cried out unto the LORD.**
EXODUS 14:10

Quiz 7

Good afternoon. I was a foreigner who held an important office in my sovereign's cabinet. A Christian approached me as I was reading. He gave me new understanding about the passages of the Old Testament, leading me to salvation in Christ the Lord.

I am _____.

LOST AND FOUND

▶▶   1. The passage on the Ethiopian eunuch is found in what book of the Bible?

▶▶   2. True or False: Philip was led to travel, to Gaza near Jerusalem, by an angel of the Lord.

▶▶   3. During the time my story takes place, the ruler of Ethiopia was:

       a. Ramses
       b. Candace
       c. Xerxes
       d. Agrippa

▶▶   4. The eunuch was:

       a. head of the king's harem
       b. the treasurer
       c. the king's cupbearer
       d. the court jester

▶▶ 5. True or False: The eunuch's name was Eustis.

▶▶ 6. Why had the eunuch been to Jerusalem?

▶▶ 7. When the Spirit led Philip to join the eunuch, the eunuch was:

    a. asleep
    b. eating
    c. sitting in his chariot
    d. counting money

▶▶ 8. True or False: The eunuch was reading the Book of Isaiah, often referred to in the King James Version as the prophet Esaias.

▶▶ 9. *And Philip ran thither to him, and heard him read the prophet Esaias, and said, _____ thou what thou readest?*

▶▶ 10. True or False: The eunuch admitted he didn't comprehend what he was reading.

▶▶ 11. Philip showed the eunuch that the passages pointed to whom?

▶▶ 12. The eunuch asked to:

   a. return to Jerusalem with Philip
   b. meet Paul
   c. visit the tomb from where Jesus arose
   d. be baptized

▶▶ 13. Did Philip agree to the eunuch's request?

▶▶ 14. *And Philip said, If thou believest with all _____ _____, thou mayest. And he answered and said, I believe that Jesus Christ is the Son of God.*

▶▶ 15. After Philip's encounter with the eunuch, Philip:

a. was caught up by the Spirit of the Lord
b. was found at Azotus
c. preached in all the cities until he came to Caesarea
d. all of the above

QUIZ 7 ANSWERS

I am the Ethiopian eunuch.

1. Acts, chapter 8:26–40
2. True (Acts 8:26)
3. b. Candace (Acts 8:27)
4. b. the treasurer (Acts 8:27)
5. False. The Bible does not tell us his name.
6. He had been worshiping God (Acts 8:27).
7. c. sitting in his chariot (Acts 8:29)
8. True (Acts 8:30)
9. Understandest (Acts 8:30)
10. True (Acts 8:31)
11. Jesus (Acts 8:31–35)
12. d. be baptized (Acts 8:36)
13. Yes (Acts 8:38)
14. Thine heart (Acts 8:37)
15. d. all of the above (Acts 8:39–40)

QUIZ 7 WRAP-UP

So, how well did you know my story? Answering at least twelve questions correctly allows you to resume your travels. Look now—a king who walks with God approaches. He has a lesson to teach you from his experiences in life. May you find what you are searching for on your journey. Farewell!

I believe that Jesus Christ is the Son of God.
ACTS 8:37

Quiz 8

Shalom. The Bible records my victories in battle, my mercy to my greatest earthly enemy, my greatness—even my failures—from the time I was young to my death. I was a man of God but allowed my desire for a beautiful woman to lead me into immense sin. For a time I was lost—off of God's righteous path—and He punished me. But I returned to God and walked with Him for the remaining days of my life.

I am King _____.

▶▶ 1. We learn about David's sin in what book of the Bible?

▶▶ 2. True or False: David was not yet king when he committed the greatest sin of his life.

▶▶ 3. What country were the Israelites fighting when David's sin occurred?

▶▶ 4. When David first saw the beautiful Bathsheba, he was in:

   a. Egypt
   b. Canaan
   c. Jerusalem
   d. Nazareth

▶▶ 5. True or False: David's adultery caused Bathsheba to become pregnant.

▶▶ 6. To keep the adultery a secret, David
      sent Bathsheba's husband:

      a. home so he would lie with his wife,
         then think he was the child's father
      b. on a military mission that David
         knew would be fatal
      c. neither
      d. both

▶▶ 7. *And when the mourning was past, David*
      sent and fetched her to his house, and she
      became his wife, and bare him a son. But
      the thing that David had done
      _____ *the* LORD.

▶▶ 8. What is the name of the prophet God
      sent to David to confront him about
      this sin?

▶▶   9. True or False: After the prophet told a story about a man who had committed a great sin, David eventually realized he was the man in the story.

▶▶   10. *Now therefore the _____ shall never depart from thine house; because thou hast despised me, and hast taken the wife of Uriah the Hittite to be thy wife.*

▶▶   11. God said he would raise evil from:

        a. Ammon
        b. Judah
        c. David's own house
        d. Uriah the Hittite's house

▶▶   12. True or False: God promised David that he would not die as punishment for this sin.

▶▶ 13. The one who would die for this sin
   was:

     a. the baby conceived in adultery
     b. Bathsheba
     c. Nathan
     d. David's servant

▶▶ 14. The Bible says that God had a special
   reason for punishing this sin. What
   was it?

▶▶ 15. After this punishment, David married
   Bathsheba and a son was born. What
   was his name?

QUIZ 8 ANSWERS

I am King David.

1. 2 Samuel
2. False
3. The children of Ammon, in the country of Rabbah (2 Samuel 11:1)
4. c. Jerusalem (2 Samuel 11:1–2)
5. True (2 Samuel 11:5)
6. d. both (2 Samuel 12: 6–17)
7. Displeased (2 Samuel 11:27)
8. Nathan (2 Samuel 12:1)
9. True. The story appears in 2 Samuel 12:1–13.
10. Sword (2 Samuel 12:10)
11. c. David's own house (2 Samuel 12:11)
12. True (2 Samuel 12:13)
13. a. the baby conceived in adultery (2 Samuel 12:14)
14. The sin had given enemies of the Lord occasion to blaspheme (2 Samuel 12:14).
15. Solomon (2 Samuel 12:24)

QUIZ 8 WRAP-UP

Always be on your guard! If I could fall away from the Lord, anyone can! But anyone can be restored, too. Behold, I see a former thief approaching. His test will show you how Jesus can bring even a criminal onto the right path. I wish you well.

The LORD also hath put away thy sin; thou shalt not die.
2 SAMUEL 12:13

Quiz 9

Greetings! I was a lost sinner right up until my death. But as I was dying, Jesus told me I would be with Him in paradise.

I am a _____

on a _____.

▶▶ 1. True or False: Scriptures mentioning
       the criminal crucified with Christ are
       found in all four gospels.

▶▶ 2. Matthew says that the criminals cruci-
       fied with Christ were:

       a. murderers
       b. tax collectors
       c. thieves
       d. all of the above

▶▶ 3. Mark tells us the criminals:

       a. were both saved
       b. reviled Jesus
       c. were Gentiles
       d. witnessed the stoning of Stephen

▶▶ 4. According to the Gospel of Luke, what
       did the sign above Jesus' head say?

▶▶ 5. According to Luke, in how many languages was the sign written?

▶▶ 6. *Then said Jesus, Father, _____ them; for they know not what they do.*

▶▶ 7. The unrepentant criminal asked Jesus to:

    a. turn stones into bread
    b. ask a centurion for a cup of water
    c. bless him and his family
    d. save himself and them

▶▶ 8. In asking for this, the unrepentant criminal was asking Jesus to prove what?

▶▶ 9. *But the other answering rebuked him, saying, Dost not thou fear _____, seeing thou art in the same condemnation?*

▶ ▶ 10. True or False: The repentant criminal could see he was being justly punished.

▶ ▶ 11. The criminals are identified only as "others" in which Gospel?

▶ ▶ 12. True or False: Both criminals thought Jesus was guilty of the crimes with which He was charged.

▶ ▶ 13. The repentant criminal asked Jesus to:

   a. remember him
   b. reward him for defending Him against the other criminal
   c. save him
   d. be buried with him

▶▶ 14. *And Jesus said unto him, Verily I say unto thee, _____ shalt thou be with me in paradise.*

▶▶ 15. Why didn't Jesus save both of the criminals?

QUIZ 9 ANSWERS

I am a criminal on a cross.

1. True (Matthew 27:38–44; Mark 15:27–32;
   Luke 23:32–43; John 19:18)
2. c. thieves (Matthew 27:44)
3. b. reviled Jesus (Mark 15:32)
4. THIS IS THE KING OF THE JEWS (Luke 23:38)
5. Three: Greek, Latin, and Hebrew (Luke 23:38)
6. Forgive (Luke 23:34)
7. d. save himself and them (Luke 23:39)
8. That he is the Christ (Luke 23:39)
9. God (Luke 23:40)
10. True (Luke 23:41)
11. John (John 19:18)
12. False (Luke 23:41)
13. a. remember him (Luke 23:42)
14. Today (Luke 23●43)
15. The first criminal didn't ask. We must accept Jesus
    Christ as our personal Lord and Savior if we are to
    make the leap from lost sinner to a servant who is
    found.

Quiz 9 Wrap-up

Were you able to answer at least twelve of my questions? I hope so—you don't want to hang around these crosses too long! Over the hills I see a man approaching. I've heard that he has an important lesson to teach you. Go, and find out who he is.

**For all have sinned,
and come short of the glory of God.**
ROMANS 3:23

Quiz 10

Good morning. I was a very rich man, but I did not gain my all my money honestly. My fellow citizens reviled me. I was lost, but when Jesus came to preach in my town, I wanted to see Him. After I found the saving grace of Christ the Lord, I immediately became a changed man.

I am _____.

LOST AND FOUND

▶▶   1. The story of Zacchaeus is found in:

      a. Matthew   c. neither
      b. Luke   d. both

▶▶   2. Jesus met Zacchaeus as He passed
       through:

      a. Jerusalem   c. Bethlehem
      b. Nazareth   d. Jericho

▶▶   3. Zacchaeus was a:

      a. priest   c. prophet
      b. publican   d. false prophet

▶▶   4. As Jesus passed by, Zacchaeus was
       unable to see Him. Why?

▶▶ 5. True or False: Zacchaeus climbed into a
sycamore tree to see Jesus.

▶▶ 6. *And when Jesus came to the place, he
looked up, and saw him, and said unto
him, Zacchaeus, make haste, and come
down; for to day I must abide at thy*

_____.

▶▶ 7. True or False: The Bible says that Jesus
was able to call Zacchaeus by name because Peter had told Jesus all about him.

▶▶ 8. Jesus' words made Zacchaeus:

a. angry   c. joyful
b. frightened   d. speak in tongues

▶▶ 9. True or False: The crowds were pleased
by the prospect of Jesus dining with
Zacchaeus.

▶▶ 10. People among the crowd said Zacchaeus was:

     a. a fine man
     b. a learned rabbi
     c. wealthy enough to impress Jesus
     d. a sinner

▶▶ 11. True or False: Zacchaeus said he would give half of his goods to the poor.

▶▶ 12. Zacchaeus said he would return any stolen money:

     a. twofold
     b. fourfold
     c. tenfold
     d. a hundredfold

▶▶ 13. True or False: Jesus doubted the sincerity of Zacchaeus' repentance.

▶▶   14. True or False: Zacchaeus was a Gentile.

▶▶   15. *For the Son of man is come to seek and to
        save that which was _____.*

QUIZ 10 ANSWERS

I am Zacchaeus.

1. b. Luke (chapter 19)
2. d. Jericho (Luke 19:1)
3. b. publican (Luke 19:2). Publicans were tax collectors.
4. He was too short (Luke 19:3).
5. True (Luke 19:4)
6. House (Luke 19:5)
7. False
8. c. joyful (Luke 19:6)
9. False (Luke 19:7)
10. d. a sinner (Luke 19:7)
11. True (Luke 19:8)
12. b. fourfold (Luke 19:8)
13. False (Luke 19:9)
14. False (Luke 19:9)
15. Lost (Luke 19:10)

QUIZ 10 WRAP-UP

So, were you able to answer sixteen of the fifteen questions correctly? Sorry—just a little tax collector's joke, there. I trust that you've learned much from my story. On with your journey, my friend. I see another traveling companion waiting in the distance.

**Make haste, and come down;
for to day I must abide at thy house.**

LUKE 19:5

Quiz 11

Shalom! I am a citizen of a city that was great in Old Testament times. My city was lost, so lost in fact, that it was doomed. Through the preaching of a fishy-smelling prophet, my people repented and were able to stop God's judgment. From where do I hail?

I am from _____.

▶▶   1. *Arise, go unto Nineveh, that* _____
     city, and preach unto it the preaching that I
     bid thee.

▶▶   2. How many days would it take a person
     to walk around the outside boundaries
     of Nineveh?

▶▶   3. How many people lived in Nineveh in
     Jonah's time?

▶▶   4. According to what the Lord told Jonah
     to say, what would happen to Nineveh
     in forty days?

▶ ▶ 5. When the king heard Jonah's message, he:

      a. arose from his throne
      b. put aside his robe
      c. sat in ashes
      d. all of the above

▶ ▶ 6. The king's name:

      a. was Nebuchadnezzar
      b. was Darius
      c. was Xerxes
      d. is not revealed in the Bible

▶ ▶ 7. Did all of the people participate in the fasting after Jonah preached?

▶ ▶ 8. True or False: The king published a decree ordering all to repent.

▶▶ 9. The sin mentioned specifically in the decree is:

     a. adultery
     b. idolatry
     c. usury
     d. violence

▶▶ 10. What reason did the king offer to encourage his people to repent?

▶▶ 11. *And God saw their works, that they turned from their evil way; and God* _____ *of the evil, that he had said that he would do unto them; and he did it not.*

▶▶ 12. Was Nineveh destroyed by God?

▶ ▶ 13. Name one of the two other Old
         Testament prophetic books that spoke
         warnings to Nineveh.

▶ ▶ 14. True or False: Jesus mentioned the
         people of Nineveh in His teaching.

▶ ▶ 15. How did Jesus compare Himself
         with Jonah?

QUIZ 11 ANSWERS

I am from Nineveh.

1.   Great (Jonah 3:2)
2.   Three (Jonah 3:3)
3.   More than 120,000 (Jonah 4:11)
4.   The city would be overthrown (Jonah 3:4).
5.   d. all of the above (Jonah 3:6)
6.   d. is not revealed in the Bible
7.   Yes (Jonah 3:5)
8.   True (Jonah 3:7–9)
9.   d. violence (Jonah 3:8)
10. That God might change His mind and they wouldn't perish (Jonah 3:9)
11. Repented (Jonah 3:10)
12. No (Jonah 3:10)
13. Nahum (1:1) and Zephaniah (2:13)
14. True (Matthew 12:41, Luke 11:32)
15. "Greater than" Jonah (Matthew 12:41)

QUIZ 11 WRAP-UP

Were you able to answer at least twelve of my questions? I hope so—the entire city of Nineveh is cheering you on! But look—a Roman governor is on his way to quiz you next. Peace to you.

**I cried by reason of
mine affliction unto the LORD,
and he heard me.**
JONAH 2:2

Quiz 12

I was a Roman governor in the time of Paul the Apostle. Like all men who were faithful to Rome, I was lost to the true Lord, Jesus Christ.

When Paul was brought to me for a fair hearing regarding his offenses, I set him in chains. Paul took the opportunity to witness about the Lord Jesus Christ to my wife and me. That day, I heard the gospel message.

My name is _____.

▶▶ 1. Where is the incident with Felix recorded in the Bible?

▶▶ 2. Does the Bible mention anyone else named Felix?

▶▶ 3. Felix was governor of:

a. Judea   c. Jerusalem
b. Caesarea   d. Rome

▶▶ 4. Paul was sent to Felix by:

a. Claudius Lysias, a Roman soldier
b. King Agrippa
c. Caesar
d. Porcius Festus, Roman governor of Antioch

▶▶ 5. True or False: Because he was taken to Felix, Paul was rescued from certain death at the hands of more than forty Jews who opposed his teachings.

▶▶ 6. How did Paul know he was to take the gospel to Rome?

▶▶ 7. *And have hope toward God, which they themselves also allow, that there shall be a _____ of the dead, both of the just and unjust.*

▶▶ 8. True or False: Felix was married to a Jewess named Drusilla.

▶▶ 9. When Paul told Felix and his wife about Jesus' coming judgment, Felix:

    a. scoffed
    b. called for Paul's execution
    c. immediately worshiped Jesus
    d. trembled

▶▶ 10. True or False: Felix told Paul to go his way, and Felix would call for him at his convenience.

▶▶ 11. Felix hoped Paul would:

    a. bribe him
    b. use his influence to gain Felix favor with the Jews
    c. summon Jesus to appear
    d. escape

▶▶ 12. Paul and Felix talked intermittently for how many years?

▶▶ 13. Felix left Paul's case for the next governor because he wanted to gain favor with:

a. the king
b. the Jews
c. his wife's prominent family
d. the Christians

▶▶ 14. True or False: Eager to see their leader leave prison, Philemon secretly bribed the next governor to secure Paul's release.

▶▶ 15. True or False: By obeying God, Paul was able to take his testimony about the saving grace of Jesus Christ to two Roman governors and a king.

QUIZ 12 ANSWERS

My name is Felix.

1. Acts, chapters 23–25
2. No
3. b. Caesarea (Acts 23:23)
4. a. Claudius Lysias, a Roman soldier (Acts 23:26)
5. True (Acts 23:12–13)
6. *And the night following the Lord stood by him, and said, Be of good cheer, Paul: for as thou hast testified of me in Jerusalem, so must thou bear witness also at Rome.* (Acts 23:11)
7. Resurrection (Acts 24:15)
8. True (Acts 24:24)
9. d. trembled (Acts 24:25)
10. True (Acts 24:25)
11. a. bribe him (Acts 24:26)
12. Two (Acts 24:27)
13. b. the Jews (Acts 24:27)
14. False
15. True. Read all about Paul's time in Caesarea in Acts, chapters 23–27.

QUIZ 12 WRAP-UP

Now I must return to my official duties—so I leave you to your next test. You will learn much about your God's mercy from the woman who is now approaching.

**So worship I the God of my fathers,
believing all things which are written
in the law and in the prophets.**

ACTS 24:14

Quiz 13

Shalom. I am the sister of an Old Testament patriarch. Although I was a woman of God, I sinned by speaking against my brother. The Lord punished me as a result. Even though I sinned, the Lord showed me mercy. Likewise, He shows forgiveness to all lost people who repent of sin.

I am _____.

▶▶   1. True or False: Miriam is mentioned in five books of the Bible.

▶▶   2. Miriam was a:

    a. priestess   c. concubine
    b. judge   d. prophetess

▶▶   3. Who were Miriam's brothers?

▶▶   4. When Miriam is first mentioned by name in the Bible, she is:

    a. drinking wine
    b. celebrating the Israelites' victory over the Canaanites
    c. leading the women in song and dance
    d. predicting good tidings for Israel

▶▶ 5. Why was Miriam doing this?

▶▶ 6. True or False: Miriam credited the
         Lord for Israel's celebration.

▶▶ 7. *For the horse of _____ went in
         with his chariots and with his horsemen
         into the sea, and the LORD brought again
         the waters of the sea upon them; but the
         children of Israel went on dry land in the
         midst of the sea.*

▶▶ 8. *And Miriam and Aaron spake against
         Moses because of the _____
         woman whom he had married.*

▶▶ 9. True or False: The Lord called Aaron
         and Miriam into the tabernacle to
         chasten them for speaking against
         Moses.

▶▶ 10. The Lord:

    a. told Miriam she would die
    b. gave Miriam leprosy
    c. opened Miriam's eyes to prophecy
    d. told Miriam she would never bear a son

▶▶ 11. After he saw this, Aaron:

    a. pleaded with God for His forgiveness
    b. praised the Lord for His blessing
    c. asked Miriam to predict his future
    d. begged Moses' forgiveness

▶▶ 12. What did Moses do in response to his brother's request?

▶▶ 13. True or False: In response to Moses' request, God exiled Miriam outside the camp for seven days.

▶▶ 14. True or False: To punish Miriam, the Israelites moved on without her.

▶▶ 15. Miriam was buried in:

    a. Egypt   c. Bethlehem
    b. Kadesh   d. Canaan

QUIZ 13 ANSWERS

I am Miriam.

1. True: Exodus, Numbers, Deuteronomy, 1 Chronicles, and Micah
2. d. prophetess (Exodus 15:20)
3. Aaron and Moses (1 Chronicles 6:3)
4. c. leading the women in song and dance (Exodus 15:20)
5. To celebrate the parting of the Red Sea and exit from Egypt (Exodus 15:19)
6. True (Exodus 15:21)
7. Pharaoh (Exodus 15:19)
8. Ethiopian (Numbers 12:1)
9. True (Numbers 12:5–8)
10. b. gave Miriam leprosy (Numbers 12:10)
11. d. begged Moses' forgiveness (Numbers 12:11)
12. He asked God to heal Miriam (Numbers 12:13).
13. True (Numbers 12:14)
14. False (Numbers 12:14–16)
15. b. Kadesh (Numbers 20:1)

QUIZ 13 WRAP-UP

I pray your response to my questions was better than my response to Moses' marriage! And now another king awaits you. His quiz will show you how he repented and turned to God for peace and forgiveness. I wish you well on the rest of your journey.

**Sing ye to the LORD,
for he hath triumphed gloriously.**
EXODUS 15:21

Quiz 14

Though I was a pagan king, I loved Daniel, who served the one true God. Sadly, I nevertheless signed a decree that almost caused Daniel's death. After I saw my mistake, I turned to the God of Daniel.

I am _____.

▶▶   1. In what chapter of Daniel do we first meet Darius?

▶▶   2. Who had just died when Darius's rule began?

▶▶   3. How old was Darius when he began to rule?

▶▶   4. Daniel's peers in government were jealous because Daniel:

   a. had married the king's daughter
   b. had become the king's treasurer
   c. was being considered to oversee the whole realm
   d. he was tall, comely, and of ruddy complexion

▶▶ 5. *Then the presidents and princes sought to find occasion against Daniel concerning the kingdom; but they could find none occasion nor fault; forasmuch as he was _____, neither was there any error or fault found in him.*

▶▶ 6. Daniel's rivals convinced Darius to sign a law making it illegal to worship any one but:

a. Darius   c. the moon
b. Dagon   d. Baal

▶▶ 7. Violators of the law would be:

a. thrown to the lions
b. made to pay double in taxes
c. given twenty-four hours to flee to a city of refuge
d. burned in a furnace

▶▶ 8. True or False: Daniel was unaware of the law.

▶▶ 9. When Daniel was caught worshiping Jehovah, Darius wanted to revoke the law. Why wasn't this possible?

▶▶ 10. True or False: When Daniel was being punished, Darius wished Daniel's God would save Daniel.

▶▶ 11. Darius sealed the den with a rock and what?

▶▶ 12. True or False: Once the punishment was enacted, Darius worried no longer.

▶▶ 13. *And when he came to the den, he cried with a lamentable voice unto Daniel: and the king spake and said to Daniel, O Daniel, servant of the living God, is thy God, whom thou servest continually, able to _____ thee from the lions?*

▶▶ 14. After an angel of the Lord saved Daniel, Darius:

    a. showed mercy to Daniel's enemies
    b. threw Daniel's enemies into the den
    c. threw Daniel's enemies and their wives into the den
    d. threw Daniel's enemies, their wives, and their children, into the den

▶▶ 15. After that, what did Darius decree?

QUIZ 14 ANSWERS

I am King Darius.

1. Chapter 5, verse 31
2. Belshazzar (Daniel 5:30–31)
3. Sixty-two (Daniel 5:31)
4. c. was being considered to oversee the whole realm (Daniel 6:3)
5. Faithful (Daniel 6:4)
6. a. Darius (Daniel 6:7)
7. a. thrown to the lions (Daniel 6:7)
8. False (Daniel 6:10)
9. The law of the Medes and Persians forbid it (Daniel 6:12).
10. True (Daniel 6:16)
11. His own signet ring (Daniel 6:17)
12. False (Daniel 6:18–19)
13. Deliver (Daniel 6:20)
14. d. threw Daniel's enemies, their wives, and their children, into the den (Daniel 6:24)
15. *That in every dominion of my kingdom men tremble and fear before the God of Daniel: for he is the living God, and stedfast for ever, and his kingdom that which shall not be destroyed, and his dominion shall be even unto the end.* (Daniel 6:26)

QUIZ 14 WRAP-UP

Were you wise like Daniel and able to answer at least twelve of my questions? I pray so. Farewell, I must go now. Your next inquisitor—a man who turned from his deceit—is waiting with your next test.

He is the living God, and stedfast for ever, and his kingdom that which shall not be destroyed, and his dominion shall be even unto the end.
DANIEL 6:26

Quiz 15

Lost before Jesus called me to His service, I was one of His faithful disciples. Yet on the night of His crucifixion, Jesus predicted I would deny Him.

After I repented, another of Christ's prophecies about me came to pass when I proved instrumental in building the early Christian church.

I am _____.

▶▶   1. Although Peter was one of Jesus' disciples, he denied him how many times?

▶▶   2. True or False: Peter preached at Pentecost.

▶▶   3. *And it shall come to pass, that whosoever shall call on the name of the Lord shall be*

       _____.

▶▶   4. Peter healed Aeneas from:

     a. palsy   c. lameness
     b. leprosy   d. demon possession

▶▶   5. What miracle did Peter perform in Joppa that spread Jesus' name in that city?

▶▶ 6. Peter saw a vision that showed him it is permissible to:

    a. eat food that had been sacrificed to idols

    b. eat only animals considered clean under Jewish law

    c. be a vegetarian

    d. eat all sorts and kinds of animals

▶▶ 7. True or False: Unlike Paul, Peter refused to preach to the Gentiles.

▶▶ 8. True or False: Peter was adamant that the power of the Holy Spirit cannot be bought.

▶▶ 9. *Then remembered I the word of the Lord, how that he said, John indeed baptized with water; but ye shall be baptized with the* _____ _____.

▶▶ 10. Peter was arrested by Herod because:

     a. he wanted to please the Jews
     b. he had been bribed to arrest Peter
     c. Peter refused to worship Herod
     d. Peter was causing riots in the streets

▶▶ 11. Peter was released from prison by:

     a. an angel of the Lord
     b. Paul
     c. Jesus
     d. a Christian prison guard

▶▶ 12. How many of Peter's letters are included in the Bible?

▶▶ 13. Peter wrote his first letters to the elect in:

    a. Pontus and Galatia
    b. Asia
    c. Cappadocia and Bithynia
    d. all of the above

▶▶ 14. *As newborn babes, desire the sincere milk of the _____, that ye may grow thereby.*

▶▶ 15. Peter's second letter is about the last days and offers admonitions about:

    a. prophets who take money for their predictions
    b. counterfeit messiahs
    c. false teachers
    d. boring sermons

QUIZ 15 ANSWERS

I am Peter.

1. 3 (John 18:15–27)
2. True (Acts 2:14–47)
3. Saved (Acts 2:21)
4. a. palsy (Acts 9:32–34)
5. He raised Dorcas, also known as Tabitha, from the dead (Acts 9:36–40).
6. d. eat all sorts and kinds of animals (Acts 10:9–18)
7. False (Acts 11:1–3)
8. True (Acts 8:20)
9. Holy Ghost (Acts 11:16)
10. a. he wanted to please the Jews (Acts 12:1–3)
11. a. an angel of the Lord (Acts 12:7)
12. Two
13. d. all of the above (1 Peter 1:1–2)
14. word (1Peter 2:2)
15. c. false teachers (2 Peter 1:19–2:22)

QUIZ 15 WRAP-UP

When you feel like you've failed the Lord, be encouraged by my story—He is always ready to forgive and restore fellowship. Look! Over there. . . I see a prison guard coming this way. I wonder what he wants?

**Blessed be the God and Father
of our Lord Jesus Christ,
which according to his abundant mercy
hath begotten us again unto a lively hope
by the resurrection of
Jesus Christ from the dead.**

1 PETER 1:3

Quiz 16

Good evening to you. When I went to work that night, I figured I could catch some Zs. After all, no one was going to escape my prison, especially not harmless missionaries. Another night, another denarius.

But then, the Lord shook the prison's foundation. Not coincidently, the foundation of my pagan ways was shaken that night, too. I discovered I was lost. When Paul and Silas brought me to Christ, I was found. I began to worship Jesus Christ as the only Son of God the Father.

Paul's message is as true today as it ever was. May all lost souls hear and receive this message!

I am the _____

_____ **.**

▶▶ 1. Those who had brought charges against Paul and Silas were:

    a. temple moneychangers that Paul had assaulted
    b. centurions in the Roman army
    c. priestesses of the Greek goddess, Diana
    d. masters of a damsel possessed with a divining spirit that Paul had healed

▶▶ 2. In their prison cells, what did Paul and Silas do at midnight?

▶▶ 3. True or False: During this time, the jailer was sleeping.

▶▶ 4. Suddenly:

    a. an earthquake occurred
    b. an angel appeared
    c. Paul had a vision
    d. fire rained down from heaven

▶▶ 5. What happened after this?

▶▶ 6. True or False: As soon as this happened, the jailer planned to kill himself.

▶▶ 7. Paul told the jailer:

    a. they were innocent
    b. to make his escape with them
    c. not to worry, because they were with him
    d. he would defend the jailer in court

▶ ▶   8. *Then he called for a light, and sprang in, and came trembling, and fell down before Paul and Silas, And brought them out, and said, Sirs, what must I do to be* _____?

▶ ▶   9. What answer did they give to the jailer?

▶ ▶ 10. True or False: That night, the jailer and his house (family) were converted.

▶ ▶ 11. That night, the jailer:

      a. washed their stripes
      b. brought them to his house
      c. set meat before them
      d. all of the above

▶ ▶ 12. True or False: The Bible tells us the jailer's name was Eustis.

▶▶ 13. Paul and Silas stayed in prison until:

    a. a trial set them free
    b. the next day
    c. a year had passed
    d. the next Passover celebration

▶▶ 14. When they were freed, Paul:

    a. left quietly
    b. demanded that the magistrates release them in person
    c. asked for water and bread to sustain them
    d. asked to see Caesar

▶▶ 15. After their release, Paul and Silas:

    a. went to Lydia's
    b. comforted the brethren
    c. departed the city
    d. all of the above

QUIZ 16 ANSWERS

I am the Philippian jailer.

1.   d. masters of a damsel possessed with a divining spirit
     that Paul had healed (Acts 16:17–24)
2.   Prayed and sang (Acts 16:25)
3.   True (Acts 16:27)
4.   a. an earthquake occurred (Acts 16:26)
5.   The doors of the prison opened and their shackles
     were loosed (Acts 16:26).
6.   True (Acts 16:27)
7.   c. not to worry, because they were with him (Acts
     16:28)
8.   Saved (Acts 16:29–30)
9.   *And they said, Believe on the Lord Jesus Christ, and thou*
     shalt be saved, and thy house. (Acts 16:31)
10. True (Acts 16:31–34)
11. d. all of the above (Acts 16:33–34)
12. False: The Bible does not tell us his name.
13. b. the next day (Acts 16:35)
14. b. demanded that the magistrates release them in per-
     son (Acts 16:37)
15. d. all of the above (Acts 16:40)

QUIZ 16 WRAP-UP

Did you answer at least twelve of my questions?
Then I'll "release" you to continue your journey.
Behold! I see a woman from a pagan city
approaching. She has another test to give you. I
wish you well.

**He. . . rejoiced,
believing in God with all his house.**
ACTS 16:34

Quiz 17

Like many people today I lived among the lost, in a pagan city. Even though I was by no means free from sin, I was nevertheless a believer in the true God. I was called upon to do a favor for His people. I risked my own life to help them.

I am _____.

▶▶   1. Rahab's story is recorded in:

     a. Joshua   c. 1 Chronicles
     b. 2 Kings   d. Ezra

▶▶   2. True or False: Rahab was a prostitute.

▶▶   3. Rahab lived in:

     a. Nazareth   c. Jericho
     b. Byzantium   d. Ur

▶▶   4. The one who sent the spies was:

     a. Pharaoh   c. Saul
     b. Moses   d. Joshua

▶▶ 5. *And the king of Jericho sent unto Rahab, saying, Bring forth the men that are come to thee, which are entered into thine house: for they be come to _____ out all the country.*

▶▶ 6. What did Rahab do in response to the king's request?

▶▶ 7. The spies found themselves among:

    a. enemy spies
    b. flax
    c. members of a bridal party
    d. tares

▶▶ 8. *And she said unto the men, I know that the _____ hath given you the land, and that your terror is fallen upon us, and that all the inhabitants of the land faint because of you.*

▶▶ 9. Rahab believed in God because:

    a. she had heard about the parting of the Red Sea

    b. she had heard about the destruction of the Amorite kings

    c. she had heard about the great flood and God's promise sealed with a rainbow

    d. a and b

▶▶ 10. *And as soon as we had heard these things, our hearts did melt, neither did there remain any more courage in any man, because of you: for the* LORD *your* _____, *he is* _____ *in heaven above, and in earth beneath.* (same word in both blanks)

▶▶ 11. What did Rahab ask the spies to do for her?

▶▶ 12. Did the spies agree to her request?

▶▶ 13. Rahab's house was located:

    a. on a mountaintop
    b. on the town wall
    c. near a grape arbor
    d. just behind the entrance to the city

▶▶ 14. Rahab marked her house with:

    a. the blood of a lamb
    b. a scarlet line
    c. nothing
    d. her name in Hebrew

▶▶ 15. True or False: Because of their experience with Rahab, the spies doubted the land would be theirs.

QUIZ 17 ANSWERS

I am Rahab.

1. a. Joshua
2. True (Joshua 2:1)
3. c. Jericho (Joshua 2:1)
4. d. Joshua (Joshua 2:1)
5. Search (Joshua 2:3)
6. She hid the spies (Joshua 2:4–6).
7. b. flax (Joshua 2:6)
8. LORD (Joshua 2:9)
9. d. a and b (Joshua 2:10)
10. God, God (Joshua 2:11)
11. She asked them to save the lives of her and her family (Joshua 2:13).
12. Yes (Joshua 2:14)
13. b. on the town wall (Joshua 2:15)
14. b. a scarlet line (Joshua 2:18)
15. False (Joshua 2:24)

Quiz 17 Wrap-up

I won't let you escape until you've answered at least twelve of my questions! Now go—I see an apostle coming over the hill. He has another test for you.

Truly the Lord hath delivered into our hands all the land.
Joshua 2:24

Quiz 18

Grace to you. I am one of the twelve apostles. I was a lost sinner, a man engaged in one of the most hated professions of my time. Yet Jesus selected me to follow Him.

When Jesus chose me, I was not good enough to follow in His ways. His willingness to select me as a disciple shows that He does not expect us to come to Him in our own perfection, but to be justified by the shedding of His blood.

I am _____.

▶▶ 1. True or False: Matthew is mentioned by name in all four gospels.

▶▶ 2. The King James Version of Scripture calls Matthew a publican. What is a publican?

▶▶ 3. When Jesus called Matthew to follow him, Matthew was:

    a. sitting at the receipt of custom
    b. praying
    c. making a traditional wave offering
    d. persecuting Christians

▶▶ 4. True or False: When Jesus chose Matthew, Matthew argued that he was not yet ready to follow the Lord.

▶▶ 5. When Jesus chose Matthew, Jesus had just:

    a. forgiven the sins of a sick man
    b. enabled a man with palsy to walk
    c. showed scribes His authority to forgive sin
    d. all of the above

▶▶ 6. *And, behold, they brought to him a man sick of the palsy, lying on a bed: and Jesus seeing their faith said unto the sick of the palsy; Son, be of good _____; thy sins be forgiven thee.*

▶▶ 7. True or False: When Jesus said this, a group of scribes accused Him of blasphemy.

147

▶▶   8. Immediately after Matthew's selection, controversy occurred over:

   a. working on the Sabbath
   b. the fact Jesus was eating with sinners
   c. healing physical ailments of sinners
   d. whether Jesus' ministry is predicted in Isaiah

▶▶   9. *But when Jesus heard that, he said unto them, They that be whole need not a physician, but they that are sick. But go ye and learn what that meaneth, I will have mercy, and not sacrifice: for I am not come to call the righteous, but _____ to repentance.*

▶▶   10. True or False: At the point in His ministry when Jesus chose Matthew, the Jewish authorities were already confronting and accusing Jesus directly.

▶▶   11. True or False: Matthew the apostle wrote the Gospel of Matthew.

▶▶ 12. What is unusual about the lineage of Jesus as recorded in the Gospel of Matthew?

▶▶ 13. In the Book of Acts, we find Matthew in a meeting where he:

    a. returns to his former profession
    b. gives all his wealth to the poor
    c. prays in an upper room
    d. consoles Jesus' mother

▶▶ 14. During this meeting, a disciple is appointed to replace Judas. What was his name?

▶▶ 15. The next big event recorded in Acts is the day of:

    a. Easter   c. Christmas
    b. Passover   d. Pentecost

QUIZ 18 ANSWERS

I am Matthew.

1. False. He is not mentioned by name in John.
2. A tax collector
3. a. sitting at the receipt of custom (Matthew 9:9). This is the tax collector's booth.
4. False. No hesitation is noted in Matthew 9:9.
5. d. all of the above (Matthew 9:1–8)
6. Cheer (Matthew 9:2)
7. True (Matthew 9:3)
8. b. the fact Jesus was eating with sinners (Matthew 9:10–11)
9. Sinners (Matthew 9:12–13)
10. False. They were speaking among themselves and querying His disciples (Matthew 9:3 and 9:10–11).
11. True
12. The lineage includes women (Matthew 1:1–18)
13. c. prays in an upper room (Acts 1:13)
14. Matthias (Acts 1:25–26)
15. d. Pentecost (Acts 2:1)

QUIZ 18 WRAP-UP

Did you find my questions too "taxing"? I hope not! Now, please continue on your journey. You will next meet another man of the Bible. Farewell!

But that ye may know that the Son of man hath power on earth to forgive sins.
MATTHEW 9:6

Quiz 19

Good day to you. I was tainted by my family's worship of a false god. Then the true God commanded me to destroy the idol's altar, at risk of my own life. After I tested the Lord to be sure I was following His path, I led my people to glory.

God can work through any of us He chooses. However, before His plan for us can be realized, we must not hold false gods more dearly than Him. Some of the idols of my time were nature gods and idols made of wood or stone. Other false gods, such as love of money, power, status, and idolatry of the self, were just as prevalent in my day as they are in yours. I urge you to shed all idols and put Him above all else so that He may be glorified in you.

I am _____.

▶▶ 1. Gideon's story is found in:

      a. Judges   c. Exodus
      b. Matthew   d. Nehemiah

▶▶ 2. When Gideon was visited by an angel, Gideon was hiding wheat from the:

      a. Canaanites
      b. Jebusites
      c. Midianites
      d. Electric Lights

▶▶ 3. *And the angel of the LORD appeared unto him, and said unto him, The LORD is with thee, thou mighty man of _____.*

▶▶ 4. True or False: Gideon was not surprised when he was told the Lord would save Israel through him.

▶ ▶ 5. What god did Gideon repudiate?

▶ ▶ 6. After Gideon tore down the god's altar, the people:

   a. threw Gideon in prison
   b. vowed to put Gideon to death
   c. forced Gideon to wear ashes and sackcloth
   d. took Gideon to court for a trial

▶ ▶ 7. What man suggested that the false god defend himself against Gideon?

▶ ▶ 8. True or False: The god did not defend himself against Gideon.

▶▶ 9. Before God's plan could take place, the spirit of the Lord caused Gideon to:

    a. bang a gong
    b. blow a trumpet
    c. strum a harp
    d. sing a psalm

▶▶ 10. Gideon tested God's will with:

    a. wool and milk
    b. bagels and cream cheese
    c. fleece and dew
    d. silk and manna

▶▶ 11. What were these tests meant to show Gideon and the people?

▶▶ 12. True or False: To this day, Gideon's tests are used by Orthodox Jews to find the Lord's will.

▶▶ 13. By what other name was Gideon
       known?

▶▶ 14. True or False: The Israelites' victory
       over the Midianites was predicted in a
       dream.

▶▶ 15. After Gideon's death, Israel:

   a. remained faithful to the Lord for the
      next fourscore and three years
   b. enjoyed peace for three generations
   c. began building a temple to the one
      true God
   d. returned to worshiping false gods

QUIZ 19 ANSWERS

I am Gideon.

1. a. Judges
2. c. Midianites (Judges 6:11)
3. Valour (Judges 6:12)
4. False (Judges 6:15)
5. Baal (Judges 6:25–29)
6. b. vowed to put Gideon to death (Judges 6:30)
7. Joash, Gideon's father (Judges 6:29–31)
8. True
9. b. blow a trumpet (Judges 6:34)
10. c. fleece and dew (Judges 6:35–40)
11. That the Lord would use Gideon to save the Israelites (Judges 6:36)
12. False
13. Jerubbaal (Judges 7:1)
14. True (Judges 7:13–14). Read the details of the battles in Judges 7:15–8:27.
15. d. returned to worshiping false gods (Judges 8:33)

QUIZ 19 WRAP-UP

My guess is that you handled this challenge better than Baal handled his! If you correctly answered twelve of my questions, continue with your journey. A great leader is approaching to test you.

The LORD shall rule over you.
JUDGES 8:23

Quiz 20

I was rescued from certain death by the daughter of Pharaoh and raised as an Egyptian prince. I committed a crime and fled to a foreign land. Even with the stain of sin, I was later chosen by God to lead His people out of bondage.

I am _____.

▶▶ 1. We first meet Moses as:

     a. a baby in the bulrushes
     b. when he is first born
     c. a prince in Pharaoh's court
     d. God speaks to him through a burning bush

▶▶ 2. True or False: When he was a young man, Moses had no idea he was an adopted Hebrew.

▶▶ 3. Moses killed an Egyptian for:

     a. not pushing the slaves hard enough
     b. smiting a Hebrew
     c. smiting another Egyptian
     d. failing to bow to Pharaoh

▶▶   4. Moses fled Egypt:

      a. upon his mother's urging
      b. when Pharaoh discovered his deed
      c. after the Lord sent him a vision
      d. at his wife's request

▶▶   5. Moses gained favor in Midian by:

      a. helping sisters draw water
      b. telling the secrets of Pharaoh's court
      c. giving the citizens riches from Egypt
      d. teaching the Midianites how to build treasure cities

▶▶   6. What was Moses doing when he saw the burning bush?

▶▶   7. *And he said, Draw not nigh hither: put off thy shoes from off thy feet, for the place whereon thou standest is _____ ground.*

▶▶ 8. True or False: Moses had no hesitation
       about taking the Israelites' pleas to
       Pharaoh.

▶▶ 9. To prove to Moses the people would
       know he had seen Him, God used a:

       a. shepherd's rod   c. vision
       b. talking frog   d. golden calf

▶▶ 10. True or False: Moses protested to the
        Lord that he was slow of tongue.

▶▶ 11. Before the Israelites left Egypt, that
        country suffered how many plagues?

▶▶ 12. True or False: Moses put up resistance
        even as the Lord was working through
        him.

▶▶ 13. Obeying Moses after the last plague,
the Israelites borrowed from the
Egyptians:

a. boats to cross the Red Sea
b. gold, silver, and jewels
c. idols made of valuable metals and
jewels
d. food for the journey

▶▶ 14. To divide the Red Sea, Moses lifted:

a. the belt of his robe
b. both hands
c. the name of the Lord
d. his hand and his rod

▶▶ 15. *And Israel saw that great work which the
Lord did upon the Egyptians: and the people feared the Lord, and believed the Lord,
and his _____ Moses.*

QUIZ 20 ANSWERS

I am Moses.

1. b. when he is first born (Exodus 2:2)
2. False (Exodus 2:11)
3. b. smiting a Hebrew (Exodus 2:11–12)
4. b. when Pharaoh discovered his deed (Exodus 2:15)
5. a. helping sisters draw water (Exodus 2:19–20)
6. Tending Jethro's flock (Exodus 3:1)
7. Holy (Exodus 3:5)
8. False (Exodus 3:11)
9. a. shepherd's rod (Exodus 4:2–3)
10. True (Exodus 4:10)
11. Nine. Water turned to blood, frogs, lice, flies, murrain, boils, hail, locusts, darkness. This does not count the killing of the firstborn, under which the Israelites established Passover. For a full account, including surrounding events, read Exodus, chapters 5–12.
12. True (Exodus 6:12, 30)
13. b. gold, silver, and jewels (Exodus 12:35)
14. d. his hand and his rod (Exodus 14:16)
15. Servant (Exodus 14:31)

QUIZ 20 WRAP-UP

Have you learned from my example? God found me, a killer, and used me to lead His people—even when I resisted. What a great God He is! Behold, a woman who was lost is near to us. She is looking for you. I trust you'll learn much from the test she gives you.

Thus shalt thou say unto the children of Israel, I AM hath sent me unto you.

EXODUS 3:14

Quiz 21

I was a lost woman living in a city that professed the Lord. I was the first person Paul converted in the region where I lived. I was so grateful to Paul for sharing the gospel with me that I offered to help him and his missionary friends.

I am _____.

▶▶ 1. True or False: Lydia's story can be found in the Book of Acts.

▶▶ 2. Philippi was:

    a. a country in Asia
    b. a city in Macedonia
    c. an island in the Mediterranean
    d. a village near Bethlehem

▶▶ 3. True or False: Philippi was an insignificant place.

▶▶ 4. On what day of the week was Lydia converted?

▶▶ 5. On that day, Paul and his band of missionaries went to:

    a. a river side   c. a hilltop
    b. a synagogue   d. a garden

▶▶ 6. They went to this place to:

    a. preach   c. pray
    b. eat   d. meet other
                              missionaries

▶▶ 7. Lydia was from:

    a. Jerusalem   c. Nazareth
    b. Athens   d. Thyatira

▶▶ 8. What was Lydia's profession?

▶▶ 9. True or False: Lydia was from a province where the Holy Spirit had previously forbidden Paul to go.

▶▶ 10. Was this woman Paul's first convert in this region?

▶▶ 11. True or False: Lydia was baptized the same day.

▶▶ 12. Those baptized were:

a. Lydia only
b. Lydia and her household
c. Lydia and her neighbors
d. all of the above

▶ ▶ 13. After Lydia's conversion, she offered
Paul and his friends:

a. lodging
b. money
c. dinner
d. water for his men and beasts

▶ ▶ 14. Did they accept her offer?

▶ ▶ 15. True or False: After Lydia's conversion,
Paul's mission work in the region was
complete.

QUIZ 21 ANSWERS

I am Lydia.

1. True (Acts 16:11–15)
2. b. a city in Macedonia (Acts 16:12)
3. False (Acts 16:12)
4. The Sabbath (Acts 16:13)
5. a. a river side (Acts 16:13)
6. c. pray (Acts 16:13)
7. d. Thyatira (Acts 16:14)
8. She was a seller of purple (Acts 16:14).
9. True (Acts 16:6)
10. Yes
11. True (Acts 16:15)
12. b. Lydia and her household (Acts 16:15)
13. a. lodging (Acts 16:15)
14. Yes (Acts 16:15)
15. False (Acts 16:16–40)

QUIZ 21 WRAP-UP

Were you able to answer at least twelve of my questions? If so, you deserve a royal robe of purple! Now, a great speaker awaits your company. He has another test for you. May you learn his lesson well.

**The Lord had called us for
to preach the gospel unto them.**
ACTS 16:10

Quiz 22

Shalom, my friend. I was a great speaker. So great, in fact, that the Lord chose me to be spokesman along with my brother. We approached Pharaoh with our requests to release the Israelites from bondage. And the rest, as I understand modern people, is history!

Regrettably, I became lost for a time. I slipped off the righteous path when I approved of my people worshiping a false god, but the Lord returned me to Him again.

I am _____.

▶▶ 1. We first meet Aaron in the Bible when he is:

    a. a baby being hidden from Pharaoh
    b. speaking to Pharaoh's daughter about a Hebrew nurse for Moses
    c. writing down the Ten Commandments
    d. appointed by God to help Moses

▶▶ 2. *And he [Aaron] shall be thy _____ unto the people: and he shall be, even he shall be to thee instead of a mouth, and thou shalt be to him instead of God.*

▶▶ 3. What were Moses and Aaron commanded by the Lord to ask of Pharaoh?

▶▶ 4. True or False: Aaron was a Levite.

▶▶ 5. *And Moses and Aaron said unto all the children of Israel, At even, then ye shall know that the LORD hath brought you out from the land of _____.*

▶▶ 6. True or False: Aaron and his sons were to wear special clothing because of their position in the community.

▶▶ 7. The people became impatient with Moses to:

   a. come down from the mountain
   b. bring them the Ten Commandments
   c. lead them in song and dance
   d. gather materials to build the tabernacle

▶▶ 8. Did the people ask Aaron to make gods for them?

▶▶ 9. True or False: Aaron himself fashioned the idol and built an altar to it.

▶▶ 10. During the festival to the Lord that Aaron proclaimed, the people:

a. ate and drank
b. made offerings
c. played
d. all of the above

▶▶ 11. *And Aaron said, Let not the anger of my lord wax _____: thou knowest the people, that they are set on mischief.*

▶▶ 12. Throughout the Bible, the term "sons of Aaron" refers to:

a. priests   c. moneychangers
b. idolaters   d. all of the above

▶ ▶ 13. True or False: After his great sin, Aaron was obedient to the Lord unto his death.

▶ ▶ 14. Aaron died at:

    a. Mount Sinai
    b. the Mount of Olives
    c. Mount Hor
    d. Mount Everest

▶ ▶ 15. Is Aaron mentioned in the New Testament?

QUIZ 22 ANSWERS

I am Aaron.

1. d. appointed by God to help Moses (Exodus 4:14)
2. Spokesman (Exodus 4:16)
3. To let the Israelites out of bondage
   (Exodus 4:14–12:50)
4. True (Exodus 4:14)
5. Egypt (Exodus 16:6)
6. True (Exodus 28:1–43)
7. a. come down from the mountain (Exodus 32:1)
8. Yes (Exodus 32:1)
9. True (Exodus 32:4–5)
10. d. all of the above (Exodus 32:6)
11. Hot (Exodus 32:22)
12. a. priests
13. True (Numbers 33:38)
14. c. Mount Hor (Numbers 33:38)
15. Yes (Luke 1:5, Acts 7:40, Hebrews 5:4, 7:11)

QUIZ 22 WRAP-UP

I have enjoyed our time together, friend. May you never slip into the error to which I succumbed. I must leave you now, but I have received word that a female follower of Jesus will be arriving soon with another test for you.

**And Aaron spake all the words which
the LORD had spoken unto Moses,
and did the signs in the sight of the people.
And the people believed.**
EXODUS 4:30–31

Quiz 23

Greetings! I was a lost sinner, but the Lord Jesus Christ saved me. I became one of His many female followers. Many other New Testament women share my first name, but I am always referred to by two names.

I am _____

_____.

▶ ▶   1. True or False: Mary Magdalene is mentioned in all four Gospels.

▶ ▶   2. True or False: Mary Magdalene was present at the crucifixion of Jesus Christ.

▶ ▶   3. Does Matthew tell us that Mary Magdalene witnessed Jesus' burial?

▶ ▶   4. Matthew says Mary Magdalene was:

    a. the sister of Lazarus
    b. the sister of Martha
    c. a seller of purple
    d. a women who ministered to Christ

▶ ▶   5. Jesus had helped Mary Magdalene by:

    a. curing her of a blood disorder
    b. casting seven demons from her
    c. keeping her from being stoned
    d. healing her of leprosy

▶▶ 6. True or False: Luke says that Mary Magdalene was one of the women who sustained Jesus financially.

▶▶ 7. When Mary Magdalene first saw the empty tomb, she:

a. rejoiced   c. questioned the guards
b. was angry   d. wept

▶▶ 8. When Mary Magdalene and the other Mary went to the tomb on the Sabbath, they witnessed:

a. an earthquake
b. the appearance of an angel
c. the transfiguration
d. a and b

▶▶ 9. When Mary Magdalene first saw the risen Christ, she believed He was:

    a. an angel
    b. the gardener
    c. a disciple playing a prank
    d. John the Baptist

▶▶ 10. *And go quickly, and tell his disciples that he is _____ from the dead; and, behold, he goeth before you into Galilee; there shall ye see him: lo, I have told you.*

▶▶ 11. Who said the words in question 10?

▶▶ 12. The women had visited Jesus' tomb to:

    a. see if He had risen as promised
    b. anoint His body
    c. appease Thomas's doubt
    d. celebrate Easter

▶▶ 13. Who did Mary Magdalene and the other women tell about Jesus' resurrection?

▶▶ 14. No one believed the women were telling the truth about the resurrection until:

    a. the archangel Michael appeared and confirmed their story
    b. the guards at the tomb confirmed the story
    c. Peter saw the empty linens in the tomb
    d. Thomas placed his hand in Jesus' wound

▶▶ 15. *Jesus saith unto* [Mary Magdalene], *Touch me not; for I am not yet _____ to my Father: but go to my brethren, and say unto them, I ascend unto my Father, and your Father; and to my God, and your God.*

QUIZ 23 ANSWERS

I am Mary Magdalene.

1. True
2. True (Matthew 27:56)
3. Yes (Matthew 27:61)
4. d. one of many women who ministered to Christ (Matthew 27:55)
5. b. casting seven demons from her (Mark 16:9)
6. True (Luke 8:1–3)
7. d. wept (John 20:11)
8. d. a and b (Matthew 28:2–3)
9. b. the gardener (John 20:15)
10. Risen (Matthew 28:7)
11. The angel at the tomb (Matthew 28:2–7)
12. b. anoint his body (Mark 16:1)
13. The eleven apostles (Luke 24:10)
14. c. Peter saw the empty linens in the tomb (Luke 24:12)
15. Ascended (John 20:17–18)

QUIZ 23 WRAP-UP

Did you get past my questions? From a woman with a questionable past, I know how God can turn a life around. Peace to you on the rest of your journey. I see the friend of a king coming to see you now. Farewell.

**Mary Magdalene came
and told the disciples that
she had seen the Lord.**
JOHN 20:18

Quiz 24

Shalom. I was the best friend of a future king, much to my father's displeasure. Ultimately, I chose my friend over my father. Though I mourned when my father fell away from God, I chose to remain obedient to the Lord. Perhaps people you love, maybe even friends and family, are lost. Resist the temptation to change God's Word to pacify them. Instead, pray that He will reach them according to His will.

I am _____.

▶▶ 1. Who was Prince Jonathan's father?

▶▶ 2. Throughout the portion of Scripture containing Jonathan's story, the Bible tells us that Jonathan was:

a. valiant in battle   c. lame

b. comely   d. conceived in his father's adultery

▶▶ 3. *And Jonathan said to the young man that bare his armour, Come, and let us go over unto the garrison of these uncircumcised: it may be that the _____ will work for us: for there is no restraint to the _____ to save by many or by few.*

▶▶ 4. The uncircumcised in the verse above are the:

a. Egyptians   c. Romans

b. Canaanites   d. Philistines

▶▶ 5. Jonathan disobeyed his father's orders by:

    a. eating honey
    b. working on the Sabbath
    c. marrying a Philistine woman
    d. worshiping the god Dagon

▶▶ 6. When Jonathan was to be executed for his disobedience, he was saved by:

    a. his mother   c. the people
    b. King David   d. Samson

▶▶ 7. David, Jonathan's friend, was en-dangered by:

    a. Saul's envy
    b. flying arrows
    c. the treachery of the woman he loved
    d. jealous royal courtiers

▶▶   8. True or False: Jonathan was the one
       who told David he was in danger.

▶▶   9. *But Jonathan Saul's son* _____
       much in David: and Jonathan told David,
       saying, Saul my father seeketh to kill thee:
       now therefore, I pray thee, take heed to thy-
       self until the morning, and abide in a secret
       place, and hide thyself.

▶▶ 10. What did Jonathan do with David?

       a. fasted and prayed
       b. composed a mournful psalm
       c. made a covenant
       d. prepared a will

▶▶ 11. True or False: Saul soon realized that
       Jonathan wanted David to be the next
       king.

▶▶ 12. An angry Saul:

      a. vowed to kill David
      b. nearly killed Jonathan
      c. angered Jonathan
      d. all of the above

▶▶ 13. After this happened, Jonathan:

      a. apologized to his father
      b. made a covenant with the Lord
      c. became angry with David
      d. helped David escape

▶▶ 14. True or False: David kept his promise to Jonathan after Jonathan's death.

▶▶ 15. After Jonathan's death, what person always ate at David's table?

Quiz 24 Answers

I am Jonathan.

1. Saul (1 Samuel 14:1)
2. a. valiant in battle
3. Lord, Lord (1 Samuel 14:6)
4. d. Philistines (1 Samuel 14:4)
5. a. eating honey (1 Samuel 14:27)
6. c. the people (1 Samuel 14:45)
7. a. Saul's envy (1 Samuel 18:9)
8. True (1 Samuel 19:2)
9. Delighted (1 Samuel 19:2)
10. c. made a covenant (1 Samuel 20:16)
11. True (1 Samuel 20:30)
12. d. all of the above (1 Samuel 20:32–34)
13. d. helped David escape (1 Samuel 20:19–42)
14. True (2 Samuel 9:1)
15. Jonathan's crippled son, Mephibosheth
    (2 Samuel 9:13)

QUIZ 24 WRAP-UP

I lost my life but kept my honor—how did you do with my questions? If you answered at least twelve correctly, continue on your way. I see a Nazarite coming to speak with you.

Let us draw near hither unto God.
1 SAMUEL 14:36

Quiz 25

I was a man of God, a Nazarite. Yet I allowed my carnal weaknesses, especially my love for unworthy women, to destroy me. They led me astray, so that I was lost to the Lord. I did find Him again, even though I was blind by that time. I gave my life in destroying His enemies.

I am _____.

LOST AND FOUND

▶▶ 1. Samson's story can be found in:

   a. The Acts of the Apostles
   b. Judges
   c. 2 Kings
   d. 2 Chronicles

▶▶ 2. True or False: Samson's parents were pleased by his marriage to a Philistine woman.

▶▶ 3. Samson killed a lion with:

   a. his bare hands
   b. a slingshot
   c. a sword
   d. the jaw of a jackass

▶▶ 4. After Samson killed the lion, he later found what edible substance inside its carcass?

▶▶ 5. To avenge himself over the loss of his wife, Samson:

   a. took one hundred Philistine foreskins to his king
   b. burned the Philistines' corn
   c. destroyed the statue of the Philistine god, Dagon
   d. killed the Philistine king with a sword

▶▶ 6. What happened when the Jews bound Samson as punishment, planning to turn him over to the Philistines?

▶▶ 7. True or False: Samson killed one thousand Philistines with his bare hands.

▶▶ 8. When enemies tried to kill Samson in Gaza, he:

    a. blew a horn until the city walls fell
    b. killed the enemies with the jaw of a jackass
    c. took Delilah hostage
    d. carried away the city gate

▶▶ 9. What secret of Samson's were his enemies eager to discover?

▶▶ 10. True or False: The enemies bribed Samson's girlfriend, Delilah, with eleven hundred pieces of silver each to tell them Samson's secret.

▶▶ 11. *That he told her all his heart, and said unto her, There hath not come a razor upon mine head; for I have been a _____ unto God from my mother's womb: if I be shaven, then my strength will go from me, and I shall become weak, and be like any other man.*

▶▶ 12. True or False: Samson's capture caused the Philistines to praise Jehovah.

▶▶ 13. *And _____ called unto the Lord, and said, O Lord God, remember me, I pray thee, and strengthen me, I pray thee, only this once, O God, that I may be at once avenged of the Philistines for my two eyes.*

▶▶ 14. In order to kill three thousand Philistines, Samson:

    a. destroyed the pillars of a crowded house, causing its collapse
    b. enlisted the help of the Israelite army
    c. turned his staff into many poisonous serpents that bit them
    d. picked up the city gate and swung it at them

▶▶ 15. True or False: Samson prayed to die along with the Philistines.

QUIZ 25 ANSWERS

I am Samson.

1. b. Judges
2. False (Judges 14:3)
3. a. his bare hands (Judges 14:5–6)
4. Honey (Judges 14:8)
5. b. burned the Philistines' corn (Judges 15:1–10)
6. The spirit of the Lord loosed the bonds.
   (Judges 15:14)
7. False (Judges 15:15)
8. d. carried away the city gate (Judges 16:2–3)
9. The source of his strength (Judges 16:5)
10. True (Judges 16:5)
11. Nazarite (Judges 16:17)
12. False (Judges 16:24)
13. Samson (Judges 16:28)
14. a. destroyed the pillars of a crowded house, causing its collapse (Judges 16:29)
15. True (Judges 16:30)

Quiz 25 Wrap-up

Were you strong enough to answer at least twelve of my questions? Now I must be on my way. I wish you well on your next test. Go and meet the woman walking this way.

**And Samson called unto the Lord and said,
O Lord God, remember me, I pray thee,
and strengthen me, I pray thee, only this once.**
Judges 16:28

Quiz 26

I was a woman who took a chance. Though a sinner, I dared to approach Jesus, a revered teacher, and performed a daring act. My reward was to have my sins forgiven. I was no longer lost! Hallelujah!

I am the woman who _____

_____ & _____.

LOST AND FOUND

▶▶   1. When the woman approached Jesus, He
        was at the home of a:

        a. Pharisee
        b. tax collector
        c. prostitute
        d. sister of Lazarus

▶▶   2. What was the name of Jesus' host?

▶▶   3. At the time, He was:

        a. preaching   c. eating
        b. healing   d. praying

▶▶   4. From what city did the woman hail?

▶▶   5. We know the box she carried was
        expensive because it was made of what?

▶▶   6. What was in the box?

▶▶   7. She:

   a. washed His feet with her tears
   b. wiped His feet with her hair
   c. anointed His feet with ointment
   d. all of the above

▶▶   8. What part of the body is usually
       anointed?

▶▶   9. *Now when the Pharisee which had bidden
       him saw it, he spake within himself, say-
       ing, This man, if he were a prophet, would
       have known who and what manner of
       woman this is that toucheth him: for she is
       a* _____*.*

211

▶ ▶ 10. In response to the Pharisee's objections,
Jesus told the parable of the:

a. householder   c. harsh judge
b. lost coin   d. creditor

▶ ▶ 11. True or False: Jesus told His host,
Simon, that he had treated Him much
better than the woman had.

▶ ▶ 12. *And he said unto her, Thy sins are*

_____.

▶ ▶ 13. True or False: Jesus explained to the
men that the woman loved much
because her sins were many.

▶ ▶ 14. True or False: At this time, those who
ate with Jesus questioned who He was.

▶ ▶ 15. *And he said to the woman, Thy faith hath saved thee; go in _____.*

QUIZ 26 ANSWERS

I am the woman who anointed Jesus' feet.

1. a. Pharisee (Luke 7:36)
2. Simon (Luke 7:44)
3. c. eating (Luke 7:36)
4. Nain (Luke 7:11)
5. Alabaster (Luke 7:37)
6. Ointment (Luke 7:37)
7. d. all of the above (Luke 7:38)
8. The head (1 Samuel 10:1)
9. Sinner (Luke 7:39)
10. d. creditor (Luke 7:41–47)
11. False (Luke 7:44–46)
12. Forgiven (Luke 7:48)
13. True (Luke 7:47)
14. True (Luke 7:49)
15. Peace (Luke 7:50)

QUIZ 26 WRAP-UP

The people in Simon's house were calling me a "sinner"—and so I was. But Jesus told me that my sins were forgiven. Praise God! Your sins can be forgiven, too, if only you ask. Your journey is almost over. Only four more tests to make it through successfully. Farewell!

**Seest thou this woman?
I entered into thine house,
thou gavest me no water for my feet:
but she hath washed my feet with tears,
and wiped them with the hairs of her head.**

LUKE 7:44

Quiz 27

Shalom. I was a prophet. Not a prophet for profit, but a true prophet of the Lord. In my lifetime, I made both friends and enemies. One of my friends was a soldier I cured from leprosy. Although I was a man of God, one who never strayed from the path, I gained staunch enemies among the lost because I delivered bad news to them. Jezebel was my worst opponent—and caused me much fear.

I am _____.

▶▶   1. True or False: King Ahab was a wise
       ruler who worshiped Jehovah.

▶▶   2. Elijah's first prophecy to Ahab was:

       a. there would be no rain for a few years
       b. there would be a seven-year famine
       c. Jezebel would be killed
       d. Baal's altar would be destroyed

▶▶   3. Why were godly people opposed to
       King Ahab's marriage to Jezebel?

▶▶   4. True or False: Though Jezebel knew
       God's prophets opposed her, she never
       would have considered harming them in
       any way.

▶▶ 5. Elijah offended Jezebel by:

      a. demanding that she worship Jehovah
      b. refusing to heal her friend of leprosy
      c. killing all of Baal's prophets
      d. siding with her husband in a dispute

▶▶ 6. True or False: After he offended
        Jezebel, Elijah fled to Beer-sheba.

▶▶ 7. Who helped Elijah in his isolation?

▶▶ 8. Jezebel killed Naboth so Ahab could
        possess his:

      a. slaves   c. gold
      b. flocks   d. vineyard

▶▶ 9. The Lord told Elijah to prophesy Ahab's:

   a. conversion to Him
   b. death
   c. successful reign
   d. loss of Jezebel

▶▶ 10. *And of Jezebel also spake the Lord, saying, The _____ shall eat Jezebel by the wall of Jezreel.*

▶▶ 11. True or False: Ahab repented of his evil ways.

▶▶ 12. How much time passed before Ahab consulted four hundred heathen prophets?

▶▶ 13. True or False: Ahab died in battle, as predicted by the Lord's prophet.

▶▶ 14. On the day of Jezebel's death, she was:

    a. thrown out of a window
    b. trod by horses
    c. eaten by dogs until nothing remained
       but her skull, palms, and feet
    d. all of the above

▶▶ 15. Elijah, a man of God, was taken to
      heaven:

    a. in a whirlwind
    b. in a chariot
    c. up a stairway
    d. by climbing a ladder

QUIZ 27 ANSWERS

I am Elijah.

1. False (1 Kings 16:29–34)
2. a. there would be no rain for a few years (1 Kings 17:1)
3. She was a pagan (1 Kings 16:31).
4. False (1 Kings 18:4)
5. c. killing all of Baal's prophets (1 Kings 19:1–2)
6. True (1 Kings 19:3)
7. The Lord and/or an angel of the Lord (1 Kings 19:3–7)
8. d. vineyard (1 Kings 21:5–15)
9. b. death (21:17–24)
10. Dogs (1 Kings 21:23)
11. True (1 Kings 21:27)
12. Three years (1 Kings 22:1–6)
13. True (1 Kings 22:35)
14. d. all of the above (2 Kings 9:30–37)
15. a. in a whirlwind (2 Kings 2:1)

QUIZ 27 WRAP-UP

Though I never fell into sin, I did get lost in fear for awhile. But, as He always does, the Lord welcomed me back—and He'll do the same for you. Do you hear that? I hear a man praying loudly. Go and see who he is.

The LORD, he is the God.

1 KINGS 18:39

Quiz 28

Some say I am lost, but I disagree! On the contrary, you are privileged to be in my illustrious presence. I am a man of God, a man of learning, a man who follows the letter of the law in every way, shape, and form. I pity those who are not like me.

I spy a group of rich noblemen approaching the temple. I must pause now to pray so that they might hear me and follow my wise example.

I am the _____

who prayed loudly in the temple.

▶▶ 1. Who told the parable of the Pharisee and the publican?

▶▶ 2. This story can be found in what book of the Bible?

▶▶ 3. A Pharisee was a:

   a. civil servant
   b. university teacher
   c. doctor of the law
   d. tax collector

▶▶ 4. A publican was a:

   a. tax collector
   b. priest
   c. soldier
   d. doctor of the law

▶▶ 5. The Pharisee thanked God that he was not:

    a. an extortionist
    b. an adulterer
    c. unjust
    d. all of the above

▶▶ 6. In his prayer, the Pharisee said that twice a week, he:

    a. fasted
    b. prayed
    c. rent his clothing
    d. sacrificed a ram

▶▶ 7. What other good deed did the Pharisee confess to in his prayer?

▶▶ 8. Why did the Pharisee feel justified in considering himself better than the publican?

▶▶ 9. True or False: The publican stood far off and refused to lift his eyes to heaven.

▶▶ 10. *The publican. . .smote upon his breast, saying, God be merciful to me a* _____.

▶▶ 11. According to the parable, which man was justified?

▶▶ 12. *Every one that exalteth himself shall be abased; and he that humbleth himself shall be* _____.

▶▶ 13. True or False: The disciple Matthew had been a publican.

▶▶ 14. True or False: The apostle Paul was a Pharisee and the son of a Pharisee.

▶▶ 15. *Pride goeth before* _____, *and an haughty spirit before a fall.*

QUIZ 28 ANSWERS

I am the Pharisee who prayed loudly in the temple.

1. Jesus
2. Luke (18:9–14)
3. c. doctor of the law (Acts 5:34)
4. a. tax collector (Luke 5:27)
5. d. all of the above (Luke 18:11)
6. a. fasted (Luke 18:12)
7. That he gave tithes of all he possessed (Luke 18:12)
8. Publicans were considered corrupt because they often pocketed a portion of the taxes they collected for the hated Roman government.
9. True (Luke 18:13)
10. Sinner (Luke 18:13)
11. The Publican (Luke 18:14)
12. Exalted (Luke 18:14)
13. True (Matthew 10:3)
14. True (Acts 23:6)
15. Destruction (Proverbs 16:18)

QUIZ 28 WRAP-UP

Who is this crazy Jesus fellow who scolds the holy and righteous Pharisees? How dare He insinuate that *we* of all people could be lost? *You*, however, seem to be sinful—please depart from my presence immediately!

**The things which are impossible
with men are possible with God.**
LUKE 18:27

Quiz 29

I was a great man. A king! Because of my pride, I
believed myself worthy of worship. God worked
through Daniel to make me see that I was lost.
Because I saw God's power through His miracles,
I began to worship Him.

I am _____.

▶▶ 1. Nebuchadnezzar, King of Babylon, conquered:

    a. Jehoiakim, king of Judah
    b. David, king of Israel
    c. Saul, king of Israel
    d. Caesar, emperor of Rome

▶▶ 2. Nebuchadnezzar wanted to teach three choice Israelite children the language and literature of the:

    a. Egyptians   c. Chaldeans
    b. Romans   d. Aztecs

▶▶ 3. King Nebuchadnezzar renamed Daniel:

    a. Belteshazzar   c. Meshach
    b. Shadrach   d. Abednego

▶▶ 4. What was the king's plan for these boys after they were trained for three years?

▶▶ 5. *And in all matters of wisdom and under standing, that the king inquired of them, he found them _____ times better than all the magicians and astrologers that were in all his realm.*

▶▶ 6. True or False: God gave Daniel the ability to interpret dreams.

▶▶ 7. True or False: King Nebuchadnezzar consulted Daniel to interpret a disturbing dream.

▶▶ 8. The dream predicted:

    a. that Daniel would not worship Nebuchadnezzar
    b. the world empires, including Christ's kingdom
    c. that Nebuchadnezzar would reign in greatness for fifty years
    d. seven years of plenty

▶▶ 9. True or False: King Nebuchadnezzar worshiped Jehovah God after Daniel interpreted the dream.

▶▶ 10. After the interpretation, King Nebuchadnezzar ordered everyone to worship:

   a. Jehovah
   b. Jesus
   c. Daniel
   d. a golden image of himself

▶▶ 11. From what punishment did God save Daniel's three friends who refused to worship Nebuchadnezzar's statue?

   a. the lions' den
   b. forty lashes
   c. the fiery furnace
   d. drawing and quartering

▶▶ 12. True or False: After King Nebuchadnezzar saw that Jehovah favored the Israelite boys, he decreed that punishment would be severe for anyone who spoke amiss about Him.

▶▶ 13. What advice did Daniel give to the king when he interpreted his last vision?

▶▶ 14. The vision came true when Nebuchadnezzar:

    a. wore sackcloth
    b. was worshiped as the greatest king of Babylon
    c. ate grass like oxen
    d. ate locusts and wild honey

▶▶ 15. *Now I Nebuchadnezzar praise and extol and honour the King of heaven, all whose works are truth, and his ways judgment: and those that walk in _____ he is able to abase.*

QUIZ 29 ANSWERS

I am King Nebuchadnezzar.

1. a. Jehoiakim, king of Judah (Daniel 1:1)
2. c. Chaldeans (Daniel 1:4)
3. a. Belteshazzar (Daniel 1:7)
4. For them to serve Nebuchadnezzar (Daniel 1:5)
5. Ten (Daniel 1:20)
6. True, as is evident throughout the Book of Daniel.
7. True (Daniel 2:1–18)
8. b. the world empires, including Christ's kingdom (Daniel 2:36–45)
9. True (Daniel 2:47)
10. d. a golden image of himself (Daniel 3:1–5)
11. c. the fiery furnace (Daniel 3:8–25)
12. True (Daniel 3:29)
13. *Wherefore, O king, let my counsel be acceptable unto thee, and break off thy sins by righteousness, and thine iniquities by showing mercy to the poor; if it may be a lengthening of thy tranquillity.* (Daniel 4:27)
14. c. ate grass like oxen (Daniel 4:33)
15. Pride (Daniel 4:37)

QUIZ 29 WRAP-UP

How well could you answer my questions? I was never a very good student myself—God showed me His truth, but I tended to return to my pride. I pray that you will be spared such a fate! And now, a man whom Jesus healed is approaching. He has a test for you. I wish you well.

Blessed be the name of God for ever and ever: for wisdom and might are his.
DANIEL 2:20

Quiz 30

Jesus healed me of an infirmity that I had from birth. I was considered lost because in my day, sickness was thought to be a sign that I, or someone close to me, had sinned.

After I was healed, local religious leaders questioned me. I confessed Jesus to them. Their response was to ostracize me.

I said it then, and I'll say it today: Jesus is not a sinner, but the Son of God. Because of Him, I am no longer lost either physically or spiritually. What Jesus did for me, He can do for you! Praise Him!

I am the _____ man.

▶▶ 1. True or False: The man had been blind from birth.

▶▶ 2. The man was:

    a. a musician   c. a beggar
    b. a priest   d. a merchant

▶▶ 3. True or False: A group of Pharisees asked who had sinned for the man to suffer blindness.

▶▶ 4. Who did Jesus say sinned to cause the man to be born blind?

    a. the man himself   c. neither
    b. his parents   d. both

▶▶ 5. True or False: The man was born blind so the works of God could be revealed through him.

▶▶ 6. Jesus said, *As long as I am in the world, I am the* _____ *of the world.*

▶▶ 7. Jesus cured the man with:

    a. water from the River Jordan
    b. only a touch
    c. water from the pool of Siloam
    d. spit, clay, and water from the pool of Siloam

▶▶ 8. True or False: This is the only case in which the Bible says Jesus cured a blind man in this manner.

▶▶ 9. To what group of people did the neighbors take the man after they saw he was healed?

▶▶ 10. True or False: The man's parents were
afraid to tell the truth about their son's
healing, because anyone who confessed
Jesus would be put out of synagogue.

▶▶ 11. *He answered and said, Whether he be a*
sinner or no, I know not: one thing I
know, that, whereas I was _____,
now I see.

▶▶ 12. True or False: The man declared that
Jesus is of God.

▶▶ 13. For his confession of Christ, the man
was:

a. forgiven by the Pharisees
b. honored for his conviction
c. put out of synagogue
d. thrown into prison

▶ ▶ 14. True or False: After this happened,
Jesus found the man and told him that
He is the Son of God.

▶ ▶ 15. The man told Jesus: *Lord, I* _____.
And he worshipped him.

QUIZ 30 ANSWERS

I am the blind man.

1. True (John 9:1)
2. c. a beggar (John 9:8)
3. False (John 9:2)
4. c. neither (John 9:3)
5. True (John 9:3)
6. Light (John 9:5)
7. d. spit, clay, and water from the pool of Siloam (John 9:6–7)
8. True
9. Pharisees (John 9:13)
10. True (John 9:22–23)
11. Blind (John 9:25)
12. True (John 9:33)
13. c. put out of synagogue (John 9:34)
14. True (John 9:35–38)
15. Believe (John 9:38)

QUIZ 30 WRAP-UP

Congratulations! You have seen your way through your journey! I trust that you have learned much from the people you have met along the way. Their stories from the Bible show how even lost sinners can have their lives transformed—and be found in the saving grace of Jesus Christ our Lord.

For the Son of man is come to save that which was lost.
MATTHEW 18:11

ABOUT THE AUTHOR

TAMELA HANCOCK MURRAY

Best-selling author Tamela Hancock Murray is pleased to add *Lost and Found* to the number of Bible trivia books she has written for Barbour. She also writes inspirational romances for Barbour, often set in her native Virginia. Tamela and her husband are blessed with two daughters and enjoy teaching Vacation Bible School together.

Other Bible Trivia Books

by Tamela Hancock Murray

BIBLE SURVIVAL

**GREAT BIBLE TRIVIA
FOR KIDS**

FUN BIBLE TRIVIA 1

FUN BIBLE TRIVIA 2

Available wherever books are sold.

Or order from:

Barbour Publishing, Inc.
P.O. Box 719
Uhrichsville, OH 44683
www.barbourbooks.com

Novellas by Tamela Hancock Murray are included in:

CITY DREAMS
RESCUE
PRAIRIE COUNTY FAIR
(To release October 2002)

**Full-Length Romance Novels
by Tamela Hancock Murray**

Destinations

The Elusive Mr. Perfect

Picture of Love

The Thrill of the Hunt

LIKE BIBLE TRIVIA?

Then check out these great books from Barbour Publishing!

The Bible Detective by Carol Smith
Solve mysteries posed by a mixed-up story using biblical characters, places, and quotations.

ISBN 1-57748-838-5
Paperback/224 pages $2.97

My Final Answer by Paul Kent
Thirty separate quizzes feature twelve multiple choice questions each—and the questions get progressively harder!

ISBN 1-58660-030-3
Paperback/256 pages $2.97

Bible IQ by Rayburn Ray
One hundred sections of ten questions each—and a systematic scoring system to tell you just how well you did.

ISBN 1-57748-837-7
Paperback/256 pages $2.97

Test Your Bible Knowledge by Carl Shoup
Over 1,400 multiple-choice questions to test your mettle, tickle your funny bone, and tantalize your intellect.

ISBN 1-55748-541-0
Paperback/224 pages $2.97

Fun Facts about the Bible by Robyn Martins
Challenging and intriguing Bible trivia—expect some of the answers to surprise you!   ISBN 1-55748-897-5
Paperback/256 pages $2.97

Available wherever books are sold.
Or order from:

Barbour Publishing, Inc.
P.O. Box 719
Uhrichsville, OH 44683
http://www.barbourbooks.com

If you order by mail, add $2.00 to your order for shipping.
Prices subject to change without notice.